DEPARTMENT OF THE NAVY
HEADQUARTERS UNITED STATES MARINE CORPS
WASHINGTON, DC 20380-0001

MATERIEL FIELDING PLAN (MFP) FOR THE MOBILE PHOTOGRAPHIC LABORATORIES (MPL) (NONAERIAL), TAM NO. B1456

DEPARTMENT OF THE NAVY
HEADQUARTERS UNITED STATES MARINE CORPS
WASHINGTON, DC 20380-0001

MCO 8420.11
SST
14 Jun 91

MARINE CORPS ORDER 8420.11

From: Commandant of the Marine Corps
To: Distribution List

Subj: MATERIEL FIELDING PLAN (MFP) FOR THE MOBILE PHOTOGRAPHIC
       LABORATORIES (MPL) (NONAERIAL), TAM NO. B1456

Ref: (a) MCO P4105.3

Encl: (1) Materiel Fielding Plan (MFP) for the Mobile
           Photographic Laboratories (MPL) (Nonaerial),
           TAM No. B1456

1. Purpose. To advise field commands of equipment scheduled
for issue per provisions of the reference.

2. Information. Enclosure (1) contains schedules, procedures,
acceptance and requirements, and information necessary to ship,
process, deploy, and sustain the mobile photographic
laboratories; thus, allowing planning time for equipment
arrival.

3. Action. Addressees are to comply with the requirements of
the reference.

4. Reserve Applicability. This Order is applicable to the
Marine Corps Reserve.

R. A. TIEBOUT
By direction

DISTRIBUTION: PCN 10210651500

      Copy to: 7000110 (55)
                8145004, 005 (2)
                7000144/8145001 (1)

1. <u>Introduction</u>

   a. <u>Source of Requirement</u>. The 1st and 2d Marine Divisions field experience has discovered that the current MPL does not provide support required to perform its mission. An acquisition coordinating group was formed to conduct a meeting to discuss acquisition strategy, configuration changes, manpower issues, and integrated logistics support for the proposed new MPL program. The decision to initiate a product improvement program (PIP) to do a one for one replacement of the existing MPL's was approved by the former Deputy Chief of Staff (DC/S) for Training now CG MCCDC (TE).

   b. <u>Points of Contact</u>

Maj. R. Hathaway,   (Subject Matter Expert) 2d Mardiv,
                           AV 484-1972/3733

Msgt. R. Sanchez,   (Project Officer) CG MCRDAC (SST-241),
                           AV 278-2886/2873

Kurdt Carruthers,   (ILS Manager) CG MCRDAC (SST-120),
                           AV 278-2547/2886

Mike Weaver,   (Project Officer) McClellan AFB,
                           (MAIEP), AV 633-5994

Robyn Fait,   (Program Support) CG MCRDAC (PSD),
                           AV 226-1177/8

Gerald Hall,   (Supply Support) CG MCLB Albany
                           (Code 838-2), AV 5632

Lynette Deitz,   (Program Support-Technical Manuals)
                           CG MCRDAC (PSD-M2), AV 226-1177/78

   c. <u>Fielding Methodology</u>

      (1) <u>General Fielding Plan</u>. Procurement action has been initiated for four of the subject systems to support the 1st MarDiv, Camp Pendleton CA, 2d MarDiv, Camp Lejeune, NC, 3d MarDiv, Camp Butler Okinawa, and 4th MarDiv, Youngstown, OH. This allowance, as identified in appendix A, will satisfy identified requirements to replace the existing combat photographic systems. The first system will be fielded in 4th QTR FY90, the second system in 1st QTR FY91, the third in 3d QTR FY91 and the fourth system in 4th QTR FY91.

      (2) <u>Method of Fielding.</u> The MPL system will be issued to the Marine Expeditionary Forces (MEF's) in support of audiovisual requirements. The MEF's will have sole control of the MPL system. Receiving commands will not be required to provide a requisition for the MPL system. Shipment of the MPL's to the receiving commands will take place approximately 30 days after acceptance testing is completed. Upon receipt, the subject equipment will be placed on administrative deadline and will

remain in such status until appropriate on-the-job training is completed. Receiving commands will ensure that all requirements for electrical, water and air-conditioner/heater support are available to conduct on-the-job training.

    d. Replaced Systems Equipment

        (1) The new MPL, will replace the old MPL, NSN 6780-772-0224. The replaced photographic equipment, minus the vans, may be held by the using units until its no longer serviceable or economical to support, at which time the unserviceable equipment will be disposed of in accordance with MCO P4400.82. All serviceable nonstandard photographic equipment held will be reported to the item manager at the CG MCCDC (T32-TST) Quantico, VA. The MPL shelters without the non-standard photographic equipment will be reported to the CG MCLB Albany (Code 838-2) with appropriate disposition instructions. An information copy will be provided to Deputy CG MCRDAC (Code SST-241).

2. System Description

    a. Administrative Information

        (1) Nomenclature: Mobile Photographic Laboratories, Combat (Nonaerial)

        (2) TAMCN: B1455

        (3) SAC: 3

        (4) NSN: TBD

        (5) Unit of Issue: Each

        (6) Unit cost: $372,781

        (7) Support Cost: $43,000 per year, per system

        (8) Equipment Density: Critical low density

        (9) Readiness Reporting: Force commanders will submit speedletter reports to Deputy CG (SST-241) MCRDAC Quantico, VA, when full operational capability is achieved, or when problems arise which preclude the item from going into service. The MPL is a controlled item, and will be reported in accordance with instructions contained in MCO P4400.82.

    b. Physical Characteristics

        (1) The MPL system consists of four vans identified as follows:

ENCLOSURE (1)

2

Van Operational Configuration

Length	240 inches
Width	96 inches
Height	96 inches
Square	160 feet
Cube	1,280 cubic feet
*Weight (van 1)	7,120 lbs 15,000 gross loaded
(van 2)	6,150 lbs 15,000 gross loaded
(van 3)	6,800 lbs 15,000 gross loaded
(van 4)	7,140 lbs 15,000 gross loaded

*The gross weight includes the van and equipment with overpacked spares and repair parts.

(2) Stowage 1,280 cubic feet 5,120 cubic feet

(3) Power Requirements. This system requires external dedicated power. Two portable generators, diesel engine driven, tactical skid mounted, 50/60Hz, 120/240V, with a capacity to operate each four shelter system and/or a smaller van configuration. The system requires those items at appendix B.

(4) Water Requirements. In addition, three portable, collapsible, water bladders with a 3000 gallon capacity each to provide van 1, van 3 and van 4 with a capacity of 7 gallons of potable water per minute are required.

c. Operational Characteristics. The MPL's are a readily transportable facility containing:

(1) Van 1: This van contains an automated color film processor with the ability to process film in high volume with the capability of processing film in sizes 110 to 220, with the capacity to process 42 rolls of 135/24 per hour; it contains an automated color print processor with the ability to process color prints in sizes from 5 by 5 inches to 11 by 14 inches, with the capacity to process 187 8 by 10 inch prints per hour.

(2) Van 2: This van contains HI8 video production equipment that will provide the capability to videotape original high resolution video, provide editing with character generator, provide the capability to view HI8 video in a field environment, and dub H18 to 3/4 inch and 1/2 inch video. Additionally this van will provide a photography administration area.

(3) Van 3: This van contains one automated black and white roll film processor with a capability to process film in sizes from disc to 16 by 20 inches, with a capacity to process 10

ENCLOSURE (1)

rolls of 135/36 per run; two enlargers, one contact printer and one print processor will maintain a capacity to process 420 prints per hour; a hand line is provided as a backup to black and white printing and film processing.

(4) Van 4: This van contains two automated roll film processors to process color slide film in sizes from disc to 16 by 20 inches, with a capacity to process approximately 40 rolls of 135/36 per hour; a slide mounter with a capacity to mount 70 slide per minute; a separate darkroom with a color enlarger is provided to support black and white or color printing.

    d. <u>Associated Systems Equipment</u>

(1) Portable generators, two per system (MEP-007A) TAM B1045, NSN 6115-00-133-9101.

(2) Tank Fabric Collapsible Onion, three per system TAM B2130, NSN 5430-01-170-6984.

(3) Environmental control units, four per system TAM B0011, NSN 4120-00-323-7780.

3. <u>Logistic Support</u>

    a. <u>Maintenance Concept</u>. The MPL will be maintained by the using unit up to and including fourth echelon level of maintenance. The echelon by echelon breakdown of maintenance tasks is at appendix C.

PHOTOGRAPHIC SYSTEM, COMBAT (NONAERIAL)

<u>MOS</u>	<u>UNIT</u>	<u>ECHELON</u>	<u>TASK</u>
4653	Using Unit	2 to 4	2 to 4
4671	Using Unit	1	
4641	Using Unit	1	1
4642	Using Unit	1	1

(1) First echelon maintenance will be performed by the operators of the commercial equipment in the using unit.

(2) Second through fourth echelons repair of commercial equipment will be accomplished by the using unit. Those repair requirements not within the capabilities of the using unit will be accomplished utilizing commercial sources.

ENCLOSURE (1)

4

Marine Corps Communications/Electronics Support System (MCCESS)
SHELTER SYSTEM

MOS	UNIT	ECHELON	TASK
4653	Using Unit	1 to 3	1 to 3
1142	Maintenance Bn FSSG	4	4

(3) First through third echelons shelter maintenance will be performed by the operators of the equipment in the using unit.

(4) Fourth echelon shelter maintenance will be performed by personnel in the Maintenance Bn FSSG, in support of the using Fleet Marine Force (FMF) units. The MCCESS Shelter Maintenance concept will be done in accordance with MCO P4105.3.

ENVIRONMENTAL CONTROL UNIT SYSTEM (TAM B0011)

MOS	UNIT	ECHELON	TASK
4653	Using Unit	1 to 2	1 to 2
1141	Maintenance Bn FSSG	3 to 4	3 to 4

(5) First and second echelons ECU maintenance will be performed by the operators of the equipment in the using unit.

(6) Third and fourth echelons ECU maintenance will be performed by the General Support Maintenance (GSM) Bn FSSG in support of the using FMF units.

GENERATOR SYSTEM (TAM B1045)

MOS	UNIT	ECHELON	TASK
4653	Using Unit	1 to 2	1 to 2
1161	Maintenance Bn FSSG	3 to 4	3 to 4

(7) First and second echelons generator maintenance is performed by the operators of the equipment in the using unit.

(8) Third and fourth echelons generator maintenance is performed by the Engineer Maintenance Company FSSG in support of the using FMF units.

b. <u>Support Requirements</u>

(1) <u>Depot Support</u>. Depot support for the rigid shelters is not required.

(2) <u>Interim Contractor Support (ICS)</u>. ICS is not required.

c. <u>Manpower, Personnel, and Training</u>

(1) <u>Personnel Requirement</u>. The T/O's listed are a realignment of the current fragmented assets in the audiovisual community. This realignment of assets is required to meet the increased demand in support by the Marine Expeditionary Force. There will be no additional manpower required to operate the MPL's. The T/O's that affect personnel requirements presently exist in FSSG, Wing, and Division assets. Appendix D shows the affected T/O's.

(2) <u>Training Requirements</u>. Selected Marine Corps personnel from 2d MarDiv with the 4653 and 4642 MOS's will be trained on operation and maintenance of commercial equipment by commercial equipment suppliers prior to first article test (appendix E). Upon completion of the first article test, selected Marine Corps personnel will be designated as a "New Equipment Training Team" (NETT) which will provide operation and maintenance training to all receiving units in conjunction with the fielding of all systems. Sacramento Air Logistics Center (SM-ALC) will provide the NETT with additional training on shelter set-up as appropriate during the conduct of the first article test. Attendance at SM-ALC is required for the NETT only. A sustainment class at SM-ALC is not required for using units.

(a) Receiving units will plan for and fund TAD for selected personnel to attend the commercial schools identified in the training requirements section. Currently, there is no tuition required for commercial vendor classes. The commercial schools identified, conduct classes continuously throughout the year. Using units are to make arrangements with commercial vendors 30 to 60 days prior to the required class. The period for attending commercial schools should be once a year or as required commencing in FY92, or until the requirement no longer exists. The technical manual, overpacked with system, will provide adequate setup information and shelter procedures.

(b) Funding for the following schools was provided by the Manpower/Training Unit at CG MCRDAC (PSL-T) for the NETT. The information provides the school name and associated TAD costs useful for TAD planning. These classes were attended as indicated by the NETT prior to the first article test. A listing of the classes attended/scheduled with associated costs are at appendix F for planning purposes.

(3) <u>Training Support Items.</u> There are no new training support items required.

d. <u>Supply Support</u>. The using unit is to have personnel trained to conduct up to fourth echelon repairs. Repair and maintenance of the commercial-type equipment if determined to be beyond the capabilities of the personnel in the using unit will be performed by local commercial contract. Third and fourth echelons maintenance repair of standard military equipment in the subject system will be accomplished by the supporting Force Service Support Group (FSSG). Appendix G shows the initial issue of spare/repair parts which will be overpacked with each MPL system. The deployment of the MPL will also require the deployment of all associated spares and repair parts originally overpacked with the system. Receiving units need to procure and maintain spare/repair parts at quantity levels received.

e. <u>Support Equipment</u>

(1) <u>Special Tools</u>. None.

(2) <u>Common Tools</u>

DESCRIPTION	PART NO./NSN
Pipe Strap Wrench	NSN 5120-00-776-1740
Thread Cutting Tap	NSN 5136-00-189-7808
Thread Cutting Tap	NSN 5136-00-237-8147
Thread Cutting Set	NSN 5136-00-596-1227
Tap & Die Set, Pipe	NSN 5136-00-357-7494
Tap & Die Set, Fine	NSN 5136-00-357-7404
Metric tool conversion kit (Jensen)	N-17DXP3
Heavy duty drill 1/2 inch	334-1
Enlarger alignment tool (Calumet)	CP9230

(3) <u>Special Purpose Test Equipment</u>. None

(4) <u>General Purpose Test Equipment</u>. One Digital Multimeter (DMM) NSN 6625-01-157-2246 has been procured and overpacked with the shelter system. The DMM will be held by the using unit for the conduct of first through fourth echelon maintenance tasks authorized by this MFP.

(5) <u>Test Program Sets</u>. None.

(6) <u>Other Support Equipment</u>. Four air-conditioner/heaters, per shelter system; three collapsible water bladders, per four shelter system, two portable generators per four shelter system, capable of operating a smaller configuration complex (one to three shelters).

f. <u>Technical Manuals</u>. Detailed operation and maintenance instructions for major installed components are included in the commercial equipment manuals provided with the system. A technical manual (TM) with a spare parts list will be published and provided for each system. One copy of the approved preliminary manual will be over packed with the first delivered system. A final manual will be overpacked with the three remaining systems and will be provided for the first fielded system. A TM S411-14/1 and SL-4-09902A will be provided for support of the basic ISO shelter.

    g. <u>Computer Resources Support</u>. N/A

    h. <u>Facilities</u>

        (1) <u>Existing Facilities</u>. Existing facilities for the old shelter system will accommodate the new shelter system.

        (2) <u>New Facilities.</u> To ensure the security of the MPL and internal components, it will require the using unit to provide a secure area and take preventive measures to protect against pilferage, damage, or sabotage of external and internal components.

        (3) <u>Interim Facilities</u>. N/A

    i. <u>Packaging, Handling, Storage, and Transportation</u>

        (1) <u>Packaging</u>. Packaging of internal components to maintain the center of gravity, and properly secure all internal equipment will be the responsibility of the audiovisual officer. The TM overpacked will provide all necessary additional guidance.

        (2) <u>Handling</u>. A brass plate attached to each shelter will contain information on height, width, length, weight, and center of gravity for each van. This plate is attached to the entrance door.

        (3) <u>Storage</u>. Using units will provide security for the MPL and its components. Storage and security of the MPL system will be the responsibility of the audiovisual officer. In addition, each van has two leveling jacks to level the van at the site. These jacks are located inside each van on the entrance doors.

        (4) <u>Transportability</u>. Each van has the capability to be lifted by crane, forklift, helicopter, and be transported by air/ rail and other surface means. The shelter is currently held certified, but will require flight test certification with the current commercial photographic equipment configuration onboard. A flight test will be conducted on the first system prior to fielding. Motor transport assets for general purpose hauling are

available organic to each division through the supporting FSSG's to assist in the transport of the MPL shelters during deployment. The vehicles identified for transport of the MPL system are the Logistic Vehicle System (LVS) MK 48/16, the Low Boy Trailer 870, and the International Organization for Standardization (ISO) configured M939 series truck. The crane and forklift capable of lifting over 10,500 lbs for moving/positioning the MPL shelters is available through the supporting FSSG.

     (5) <u>Transportability Restrictions</u>

        (a) MPL's are too large to be air transported by C-130. A C-141 and/or a C5A are capable of providing air transportation.

        (b) No more than a loaded height of 13 feet when transporting MPL's on highways.

        (c) MPL's will NOT be airdropped in any manner.

        (d) Tactical or commercial vehicles carrying MPL's will not exceed a speed of 45 MPH.

        (e) Only a helicopter capable of lifting over 10,500 lbs will be used to transport the MPL.

        (f) Only fork lifts with 8 to 9 foot long blades capable of lifting over 10,500 lbs will be used.

        (g) The MPL will not be dragged, towed, or pushed for any distance by any means.

   j. <u>Warranties</u>

     (1) All commercial photographic equipment will have the standard warranty of 90 days labor and 1 year parts upon receipt of equipment in SM-ALC Sacramento, CA.

        (a) Warranty extensions are the responsibility of the using unit. The following information is provided for budgeting purposes:

           <u>1</u> Noritsu - Extended warranty will cost $2,800 per year for the first 2 years.

           <u>2</u> Ilford - Extended warranty not recommended.

           <u>3</u> Images II - Extended warranty not recommended.

(2) FAR (46.770-5). Warranties for Government Furnished Equipment (GFE). A prime contractor is not required to provide warranties as specified in FAR 46.770-2, on any property furnished to that contractor by the United States except for the following:

(a) defects in installation;

(b) installation or modification in such manner that invalidates dates a warranty provided by the manufacturer of the property;

(c) or modifications made to the property by the prime contractor.

(3) If defects in workmanship and installation of commercial equipment are found after the MPL is delivered, the using unit will use the reporting guidance can be found in TM 4700-15/1F, Quality Deficiency Report Program.

4. <u>Actions Required to Place Equipment in Service</u>

a. <u>Gaining Commands</u>. The following actions are required to place the MPL system in service:

(1) Ensure an inventory of internal equipment is conducted upon receipt and report any missing items to CG MCRDAC (SST-241). The system will then be administration deadlined until training can be conducted by the NETT within 30 days of receipt. The using unit audiovisual officer is to plan and coordinate with the appropriate using units to ensure adequate supports are onhand to meet requirements needed to place the equipment in service.

(2) A crane or forklift capable of lifting over 10,500 lbs will be provided to move and setup the MPL system in the designated location identified by the audiovisual officer.

(3) Existing water bladders or water from a tap with approximately 7 gallons per minute flow will be provided to operate all vans that require water.

(4) Portable generators and associated support or electrical power from standard outlets will be provided to support the electrical requirements of this system.

(5) Measures to provide security for the MPL system will be implemented by the audiovisual officer.

(6) It is recommended that MPL's are placed in a level concrete or asphalt area while not on deployment.

(7) Force commanders will submit NAVGRAM reports to CG MCRDAC (SST-241) when full operational capability is achieved, and when problems arise which preclude the system from going into service. The MPL system will be a controlled item, and will be reported in accordance with the instructions contained in MCO P4400.82.

(8) To obtain supporting consumables for nonstandard equipment listed in paragraph 3d above, (while in CONUS) contact commercial vendors utilizing local supply procedures. To obtain supporting consumables for nonstandard equipment listed in paragraph 3d above, (while on deployment) contact MCLB Albany GA (Code 831-3) utilizing local supply procedures.

b. MCLB Albany. The Commanding General, Marine Corps Logistics Base, Albany, GA, will ensure the following actions are taken:

(1) The level two drawing package provided to the Marine Corps by the manufacturer (McClellan AFB, SM-ALC) are sufficient to remanufacture the system if required.

(2) The cataloging of spare repair parts have been accomplished.

(3) Establishment of depot maintenance requirements (if any) have been coordinated within MCLB Albany.

(4) Establish disposition instructions for the field disposal of the system as required.

ENCLOSURE (1)

LIST OF ALLOWANCES AND DELIVERY SCHEDULES

UNIT TITLE	NIT ALLOWANCE	ACTUAL ALLOWANCE	PLANNED FY 90 QTR 1	2	3	4	PLANNED FY 91 QTR 1	2	3	4
1st MARDIV	1	1			X					
2nd MARDIV	1	1					X			
3rd MARDIV	1	1						X		
4th MARDIV	1	1						X		

POWER REQUIREMENTS FOR DEDICATED EQUIPMENT

VAN 1

NOMENCLATURE	QTY	POWER CONSUMPTION PER KW	RATE OF USE
1. Film Processor	1	9.2	8 hrs a day
2. Print Processor	1	6.2	8 hrs a day
3. Ref/Heat Recirc	1	6.3	as needed
4. Air Compressor	1	2.5	as needed
5. Chemical Mixer	2	3.5 EA	as needed
6. Jet pump	1	.9	8 hrs a day
7. ECU	1	10.5	24 hrs a day
8. Lights	1	.8	8 hrs a day
9. Misc	1	1.0	8 hrs a day
10. Water heater	1	4.5	8 hrs a day
11. Silver Recovery	1	.2	8 hrs a day

VAN 2

1. Freeze frame/rec	1	1.0	as needed
2. Vielite	1	.25	as needed
3. Degausser	1	.25	as needed
4. Refrig/freezer	1	2.0	24 hrs a day
5. Air Compressor	1	2.5	As needed
6. ECU	1	10.5	24 hours
7. Video Equipment	1	3.5	8 hrs a day
8. Lights	1	.8	8 hrs a day
9. Misc	1	1.0	8 hrs a day

VAN 3

1. Print Processor	1	2.7	8 hrs a day
2. Film Processor	2	2.7 EA	8 hrs a day
3. Water Chiller	1	.05	8 hrs a day
4. Ref/Heat Recirc	1	6.3	8 hrs a day
5. Enlarger sys	2	.75 EA	8 hrs a day
6. Film Dryer	1	1.8	8 hrs a day
7. Air Compressor	1	2.5	as needed
8. Silver Recovery	1	.2	8 hrs a day
9. Water Heater	1	4.5	8 hrs a day
10. Vielite	1	.25	as needed
11. Jet Pump	1	.9	8 hrs a day
12. ECU	1	10.5	24 hrs a day
13. Lights	1	.8	8 hrs a day
14. Misc	1	1.0	8 hrs a day

VAN 4

1.	Slide Mounter	1	.2	8 hrs a day
2.	Film Processor	2	2.7 EA	8 hrs a day
3.	Ref/Heat Recirc	1	6.3	8 hrs a day
4.	Water Chiller	1	.05	8 hrs a day
5.	Enlarger Sys	1	.75	8 hrs a day
6.	Film Dryer	1	.25	8 hrs a day
7.	Darkroom Timer	1	.005	as needed
8.	Silver Recovery	1	.2	8 hrs a day
9.	Air Compressor	1	2.5	as needed
10.	Water Heater	1	4.5	8 hrs a day
11.	Jet Pump	1	.9	8 hrs a day
12.	ECU	1	10.5	24 hrs a day
13.	Lights	1	.8	8 hrs a day
14.	Vielite	1	.25	as needed
15.	Misc	1	1.0	8 hrs a day

DEFINITIONS

TASK 1: First Echelon. That maintenance performed by the user or operator of the equipment. It includes the proper care, use, operation, cleaning, preservation, lubrication and such adjustment, minor repair, testing, and parts replacement as may be prescribed by pertinent technical publications, tools and parts allowances. There is no requirement to collect MIMMS data at first echelon.

TASK 2: Second Echelon. Second echelon maintenance is that work performed by specially trained personnel in the organization. Appropriate publications authorize the second echelon of maintenance, additional tools and necessary parts, supplies, test equipment, and skilled personnel to perform maintenance beyond the capabilities and facilities of first echelon. This includes performance of scheduled maintenance; replacement of major assemblies/modular components which can be readily removed/installed and do not require critical adjustment; and replacement of easily accessible piece parts not authorized at first echelon.

TASK 3: Third echelon maintenance is that authorized by appropriate publications to be performed by specially trained personnel either in an intermediate or organizational role. Third echelon includes diagnosis and isolation of equipment/modular malfunctions; adjustment and alignment of modules using test, measurement, and diagnostic equipment (TMDE); repair by replacement of modular components and piece parts which do not require extensive post-maintenance testing or adjustment; limited repair of modular components requiring cleaning, seal replacement, application of external parts, and repair kits; accomplishment of minor body work and evaluation of emissions of internal combustion engines.

TASK 4: That maintenance normally associated to semi-fixed or permanent shops of intermediate maintenance activities and frequently associated to organizational shops of units with a commodity peculiar mission. Fourth echelon maintenance includes diagnosis, isolation, adjustment, calibration, alignment, and repair of malfunctions to the internal piece part level; replacement of walls defective modular components by grinding, adjusting, items such as valves, tappets, seats; replacing internal and external piece parts to include solid state integrated circuits and printed circuit boards/cards; and performance of heavy body, hull turret, and frame repair. A shelter having severe structural damage will not be repaired and must be replaced accordingly.

PERSONNEL REQUIREMENTS

GRADE	MOS	STA	OFF	ENL
WO	4602		1	
MSGT	4691			1
GYSGT	4671			1
SGT	4671			1
CPL	4671			2
LCPL	4671			5
SSGT	4653			1
SGT	4653			1
LCPL	4653			1
SSGT	4642			1
SGT	4642			4
CPL	4642			2
CPL	4641			3
LCPL	4641			4
PVT	4641			1
CPL	4641			2
			1	28

The following Table of Organizations (T/O's) and Line Numbers
will be affected:

T/O 1985G/M	T/O 1985I	T/O 1986G	T/O 1986H
LINE NO.	LINE NO.	LINE NO.	LINE NO.
25	24	0110	0012
26	25		
27	26	T/O 1986I	T/O 1988H
28	27		
29	27A	0101	0012
29A	28		
30	29	T/O 3111F	T/O 3111S
31	30		
32	31	0023	0023
33	32		
34	33	T/O 311G	
34A	34		
35	35	0023	
35A X	36 X		

T/O 8702 MWSS (FW)	T/O 8702B MWSS (FW)	T/O 8702F MWSS (FW)
LINE NO.	LINE NO.	LINE NO.
0108	0107	0107
0109	0108	0108
0110	0109	0109

T/O 8703 MWSS (RW)	T/O 8703B MWSS (RW)	T/O 8703L MWSS (RW)
LINE NO.	LINE NO.	LINE NO.
0108	0107	0107
0109	0108	0108
0110	0109	0109

Appendix D to
ENCLOSURE (1)

D-2

<u>SCHEDULE OF EVENTS</u>

First Article Buildup	Jul - Sep 90
First Article Test/Approval	Oct 90
First Article Fielding	Nov - Dec 90
First IOC	Dec - Jan 90
Second Article Buildup	Oct 90 - Jan 91
Second Article Test/Approval	Feb 91
Second Article Fielding	Mar - Apr 91
Third Article Buildup	Feb - May 91
Third Article Test/Approval	Jun 91
Third Article Fielding	Jul - Aug 91
Fourth Article Buildup	Jun - Sep 91
Fourth Article Test/Approval	Oct 91
Fourth Article Fielding	Nov - Dec 91
Fourth FOC	Dec - Jan 92

IOC - Initial Operating Capability
FOC - Final Operating Capability

Appendix E to
ENCLOSURE (1)

E-1

EQUIPMENT TRAINING COSTS

NORITSU EQUIPMENT

DATE: 13-17 NOV 89
LOCATION: BUENA PARK, CA
NUMBER OF PERSONNEL: 2
TOTAL DAYS TAD: 5
TRAVEL COST: $384.00 ROUND TRIP PER PERSON
PER DIEM: $114.00 PER PERSON PER DAY

TOTAL COST OF TRAVEL: $768.00
TOTAL PER DIEM: 1,140.00
                         _____
            TOTAL   1,908.00

Noritsu America Corporation
6900 Noritsu Ave
Buena Park, CA 90622-5039

KING CONCEPT IMAGE MAKER

DATE: 4-7 DEC 89
LOCATION: MINNEAPOLIS, MN
NUMBER OF PERSONNEL: 2
TOTAL DAYS TAD: 5
TRAVEL COST: $484.00 ROUND TRIP PER PERSON
TOTAL PER DIEM: $ 80.00 PER PERSON PER DAY

TOTAL COST OF TRAVEL: $968.00
TOTAL PER DIEM: 640.00
                         _____
            TOTAL   1,608.00

King Concept
5190 West 76th ST.
Minneapolis, MN 55435

ILFORD CORPORATION

DATE: 18-19 DEC 89
LOCATION: PARAMUS, NJ
NUMBER OF PERSONNEL: 2
TOTAL DAYS TAD: 3
TRAVEL COST: $380.00 ROUND TRIP PER PERSON
TOTAL PER DIEM: $112.00
TOTAL COST OF TRAVEL: $760.00
TOTAL PER DIEM: 672.00
                         _____
            TOTAL   1,432.00

Ilford Corporation
West 70 Century Rd.
Paramus, NJ 07653

SM-ALC SACRAMENTO CA (NETT Only)

DATE:	21-25 AUG 90
LOCATION:	SACRAMENTO, CA
NUMBER OF PERSONNEL:	4
TOTAL DAYS TAD:	5
TRAVEL COST:	$442.00 ROUND TRIP PER PERSON
TOTAL PER DIEM:	$101.00
TOTAL COST OF TRAVEL:	$1,768.00
TOTAL COST PER DIEM:	2,020.00
	_____
TOTAL	3,788.00

TOTAL: $8,736.00

SONY CORPORATION. Sony Corporation will provide training at no
cost to the Government. The training for the NETT will take
place in Camp Lejeune, NC. The following is the total cost for
the NETT training of personnel in the 1st, 3rd, and 4th
MARDIV's:

1st MARINE DIVISION

DATE:	TBA
LOCATION:	CAMP PENDLETON, CA
NUMBER OF PERSONNEL:	4
TOTAL DAYS TAD	5
TRAVEL COST:	$440.00
PER DIEM:	$101.00
TOTAL COST OF TRAVEL:	$1,768.00
TOTAL COST PER DIEM:	404.00
TOTAL COST RENTAL CAR:	150.00
	_____
TOTAL	2,322.00

3RD MARINE DIVISION

DATE:	TBA
LOCATION:	OKINAWA, JAPAN
NUMBER OF PERSONNEL:	4
NUMBER DAYS TAD	7
TRAVEL COST:	$1,698.00 ROUND TRIP PER PERSON
PER DIEM:	$126.00 PER PERSON PER DAY
TOTAL COST OF TRAVEL:	$6,792.00
TOTAL COST PER DIEM:	3,528.00
	_____
TOTAL	10,320.00

4TH MARINE DIVISION

DATE: TBD
LOCATION: YOUNGSTOWN, OH
NUMBER OF PERSONNEL: 4
NUMBER OF DAYS TAD: 5
TRAVEL COST: $344.00 ROUND TRIP PER PERSON
PER DIEM: $86.00 PER PERSON PER DAY
TOTAL COST OF TRAVEL: $1,376.00
TOTAL COST PER DIEM: 1,720.00
                        _____
           TOTAL   3,246.00

TOTAL FOR COMMERCIAL TRAINING: $ 8,736.00
          TOTAL FOR DIVISION TRAINING: 15,888.00

          GRAND TOTAL FOR TRAINING: $24,624.00

DISTRIBUTION SCHEDULE FOR PROVISIONING PROJECTS

ILFORD MG500 SPARES

	PART NO.	DESCRIPTION	QTY	UNIT COST	TOTAL COST
1.	QQ0000600	ELH LAMP	12	$ 20.24	$ 242.88
2.	QQ691P015	LINER 35MM	2	5.09	10.18
3.	QQ692P015	LINER 2 1/4"	2	5.94	11.88
4.	QQ694P005	LINER 4X5	2	6.40	12.80
5.	QQ6913101	DIFFUSER 35MM	12	1.50	18.00
6.	QQ6923101	DIFFUSER 6X7 CM	12	3.50	42.00
7.	QQ6943102	DIFFUSER NO.1 4X5	12	3.40	40.80
8.	QQ6943108	DIFFUSER NO.2 4X5	12	3.40	40.80
9.	QQ668P011	WHITE LIGHT ADAPTER	4	104.00	119.60
10.	QQ8425801	BLUE DICHROIC FILTER	4	29.90	271.20
11.	QQ8425803	HEAT FILTER	12	22.60	36.00
12.	QQ6681115	LH FILTER ARM	6	6.00	36.00
13.	QQ6682114	RH FILTER ARM	6	6.00	11.40
14.	QQ8998610	ON/OFF SWITCH	1	11.40	117.60
15.	QQ6653002	REPLACEMENT KEYPAD	1	117.60	247.00
16.	QQ6662002	POWER SUPPLY PCB	2	123.60	77.00
17.	QQ6684005	LAMP HOLDER ASSEMBLY	2	38.50	

Total: $1, 741.14

ILFORD 2150RC SPARES

	PART NO.	DESCRIPTION	QTY	UNIT COST	TOTAL COST
1.	QY0000170	2150 SPARE PART KIT CONSISTS OF:	1	$ 106.00	$ 106.00
	QY8408226	OVERFLOW O-RING	2		
	QY8408230	STANDPIPE O-RING	3		
	QY6203135	ROLLER BEARING	14		
	QY6204138	DRIVE BEARING	2		
	QY6214239	ROLLER GEAR	2		
	QY8323001	E-CLIP	2		
	QY6714127	LH ROLLER SPRING	2		
	QY6714120	RH SPRING	2		
	QY8997613	SPIRAL PIN	4		
	QY6714006	WORM-D-F	1		
	QY6714010	WORM-WASH	1		
	QN8421215	FUSE HOLDER	1		
	QJ6234178	GEAR	2		
	QJ6233114	ROLLER SPRING	4		
	QJ6234179	ROLLER BEARING	4		
	ABC	FUSE	15		

```
    --          ELECTRO LUBE        1
    --          GREASE LUBE         1


2.  QY6712025   PROC.RELAY PCB      2      732.30     1,464.00

                                          TOTAL       1,750.00


2150RC DRYER:

3.  QJ6232019   HEATER CONTROL ASSY 1      117.30       117.30

4.  QJ6233150   HEATER TUBE         3       46.20       138.60

5.  QJ6001008   CERAMIC BUSHING     8        1.03         8.24

6.  QJ6233172   HEATER CONTACT      4       10.10        40.40

                                          Total:      1,875.54
```

NORITSU 613 RA-4 SPARES

PART NO.	DESCRIPTION	QTY	UNIT COST	TOTAL COST
1. LOO-1645	SPARE PARTS KIT CONSISTING OF:	1	$ 805.00	$ 805.00
A003600	C RING, TSR#48	20		
A103753-01	GEAR	3		
A901020	HOOK	1		
A103752-01	GEAR	1		
A006105	CENTER ROLLER BEARING, TSR#13	4		
A100955-01	SPRING	8		
A116582-01	IDLE GEAR	4		
A116582-02	IDLE GEAR	4		
A006106	GEAR	1		
H010020	CONNECTING LINK, RS-25NPJL	1		
A128749	AIR FILTER	2		
A900144	HEAT GLASS (1 PC)	1		
I061053	LAMP, JCP-100V 650W	4		
B661227-01	DICHROIC REFLECTOR	2		
W401148-01	LAMP SOCKET UNIT	2		
A807771	LOWER DIFFUSER GLASS (120)	1		
A808166	DIFFUSER (135)	1		
A108630-04	SPROCKET	1		
H010561	CHAIN, RS-25NP 203L	1		

Appendix G to
ENCLOSURE (1)

A126681	MED SIZED FILTER GASKET	2
A000056/57	BLEEDER VALVE ASSY, TSR#42	2
B103977	FILTER LID	3
B103931	FILTER CASE	2
A000021	GASKET, BLEEDER VALVE, TSR#51	2
A125699-02	ELBOW FITTING VP-13	1
H010012	OFFSET CONNECTING LINK	1
L00-1103	RS-35 SINGLE LINK, H010008	1
H010569	CHAIN, RS-35 333L	1
A681852-01	LOWER TURN BELT	1
A001530	SPRING, TSR#60	2
A506305	GEAR	1
A107793-02	GEAR	1
A682778-01	SPROCKET ASSY	3
A116459-01	GEAR	3
A000776-02	GEAR	3
391-1804	UPPER TURN GUIDE, C101180	1
391-1606	UPPER TURN GUIDE, C101178	1
391-1608	GEAR, A002119	3
A506305	GEAR	2
A116459	GEAR	1
A115971	GEAR	1
A121308-02	GEAR	2
A107551	BUSHING	2
A004826-01	BUSHING SK-127-1	6
A116474-01	GEAR	2
391-1203	GEAR A114525-01	3
A500610-01	GEAR	1
A116372	BUSHING	1
A103753	GEAR	2
391-1313	GEAR A504178	1
A681669-01	GEAR	1
A681808	ROLLER ASSY	1
A681769	ROLLER ASSY	1
A119836-02	LOWER TURN ROLLER	1
A681741-02	LOWER TURN ROLLER	1
A500514	SOFT TOUCH TIRE	4
A681742-01	LOWER TURN ROLLER	1
A119836-01	LOWER TURN ROLLER	1
A681770	ROLLER ASSY	1
A681748	ROLLER ASSY	1
A508560	SPROCKET ASSY	1
A004826-02	BUSHING SK-127-2	4

```
A113932      STUD, SPROCKET        1
A114220      STUD, IDLE            1
708-1432     PRINT RIBBON
             (4/PKG)               4
H016150      BELT                  1
H030109      O RING                1
H030110      WASHER                1
H030115      NUT                   1
A681941-01   AIR FILTER            2
QSS-LUBE     6oz SILICONE GREASE   1
KB-1YN#3/4   POPPET VALVE          2
L00-0134     3M SILICONE SPRAY,
             TSR#58                1
A123546      NEW TYPE STRAINER     2
```

                                                     Total $805.00

NORITSU 450L-3-C41RA SPARES

1.   SPARE PARTS KIT
                CONSISTING OF: 1 $500.00 $500.00

```
A512874-01   RIGHT BLADE           1
A134468-01   LEFT BLADE            1
I053047      PHOTO MICRO SENSOR    1
A511115-01   TORSION BAR           1
A511116-01   TORSION BAR           1
A128749-01   AIR FILTER            1
B103578      DRIVE SPROCKET        3
A006105      BUSHING               4
A128811-01   GEAR                  2
Z009021-01   ROLLER ASSY           2
A128721-01   GEAR                  4
A128720-01   GEAR                  2
A510003      EXIT ROLLER           2
I017140      KEY BOARD             1
I012042      PUMP (PD-10)          1
W400332-12   BELLOWS PUMP          1
W400510-02   BELLOWS PUMP          1
A131129      SQUEEGEE ROLLER
             ASSY                  1
A510260-01   LEADER CARDS          25
QSS-LUBE     SILICONE GREASE
             (TUBE)                1
L00-0134     SILICONE SPRAY
             (CAN)                 1
```

                                                     TOTAL $500.00

Appendix G to
ENCLOSURE (1)

IMAGEMAKER II 8100R SPARES

	PART NO.	DESCRIPTION	QTY	UNIT COST	TOTAL COST
1.	20251	CIRCULATION PUMP	2	$ 195.00	$ 390.00
2.	11003	DIAPHRAGM	16	12.50	200.00
3.	30203	TANK VALVES (2-8)	8	55.00	440.00
4.	30203	TANK VALVES (1)	3	60.00	180.00
5.	10514	THERMISTOR TEMP DECK AIR	1	45.00	45.00
6.	10698	THERMISTOR TANK 1	1	45.00	45.00
7.	0240-0042	ROLLER CHAIN	1	16.50	16.50
8.	0226-0006	ROLL PIN	2	.20	.40
9.	20246	CRADLE MOTOR ASSY	1	350.00	350.00
10.	40090	SOLUTION RECOVERY SYSTEM	2	995.00	1,990.00

TOTAL: $ 3,656.90

GRAND TOTAL FOR SPARES FOR ONE SYSTEM: $ 9,701.68

Appendix G to
ENCLOSURE (1)